A little Book of Hope!

Unturning Stones

Anxiety
The Healing

Simone Simpson

Tellwell Talent
www.tellwell.ca

ISBN
978-0-2288-8552-8 (Paperback)
978-0-2288-9698-2 (eBook)

For Myles & Ellie.

This book was written to help heal the people of this world, to give hope and to light the path for us all to be free from anxiety.

In Memory

In loving memory of the beautiful Tia Moana,

Whose life sadly left us all too soon.

You enriched our lives with your bravery;

Your light shone through your caring heart.

Our beautiful memories stay with us,
even though we are worlds apart.

Your rainbows and sunflowers a gift for
us all, as long as we shall be apart.

In our hearts and thoughts forever,

Our love always.

IT IS BY UNTURNING every stone in our life that nothing, not one single thing, hinders us emotionally anymore! This is where you will truly find peace, truth and your beautiful authentic self!

To you:
Thank you for being brave.
Thank you for having the courage.
Thank you for taking the first step to being free from anxiety.

May this book be your hope and your light through your journey of healing from anxiety.

A calling from something far greater than myself, something that I call God, stopped me in my tracks and changed my life forever. A calling that completely made me question everything. This calling was for a special purpose in my life: to help heal and unite the world through a book; to reach out and give hope, a gift to us all.

Introduction

HOPE, INSIGHT AND HEALING! Allowing each and every one of us to understand that I believe we are not born into this world as anxious human beings. In our lives we unfortunately experience trauma in many different ways, creating anxiety within us. This anxiety is the leftover aftermath of our trauma. This trauma, left unacknowledged, untreated and emotionally not worked through, continues to live inside us, growing stronger and stronger as the years go on. We become unaware of the daily impact it has on our lives and of those around us. We become filled with insecurities, insomnia, nervousness, fear, panic, worry, loneliness, dread, despair and eventually depression, desperately hanging onto our lives at times. An emptiness, an aloneness that consumes us from within, a longing for someone—anyone— to understand it, feel it and take the pain away. The never-ending battle exhausting our minds and bodies, an internal hell! Daily we fight the battle, our internal struggle that debilitates and cripples us, leaving emotional states of physical panic and pain. I have suffered in the living hell of anxiety, a hell that dominated and controlled my life for a very long time. I worked through it, survived it and came through to other side. I was free from anxiety. I found that the greatest failings for sufferers is that there is no real hope. They have all but lost hope of being completely free from anxiety in life. We are often given ways to "manage" our anxiety through all kinds of strategies—natural remedies and more often medication—with no real hope of freedom from this cruel and personal struggle. Many self-medicate through alcohol and drugs to help numb the pain of anxiety, sadly in a losing battle.

I have asked myself a question for many years now: why do many of us suffer so much, when I know that anxiety is curable? I am living proof of it and have been free from my anxiety for a long time now. I can sincerely say, it was with commitment that I unturned every stone of trauma in my life to be free from anxiety. At times it was a confronting and emotional rollercoaster that I wished I could stop, but in the end, what waits for you is true emotional freedom: a complete release from within your very soul. The calm is the light at the end of this tunnel, a life-changing event that releases you from an emotionally crippling state that has controlled you and your life.

With all the love, sincerity and honesty from within me, it is true freedom. My calling by something far greater than myself, something that I call God, has guided me to write this little book of hope, with much love and gratitude to the very person who supported, guided and helped me through my journey of healing from anxiety. This perspicacious, enriching counsellor helped me work through, survive and reach the light at the end of this tunnel. I am forever grateful and sincerely humbled to have had such a beautifully authentic human being walk by my side until the very end. My words will never express how incredibly blessed I feel for your wisdom, insight and ongoing support, encouraging me to always find my truth in this life.

Love and gratitude always

Dedicated to You All

MY EMPATHY AND COMPASSION to reach out and help people still living with the struggle of anxiety is my true purpose and calling for this book. To this day I still live in an authentically beautiful state of blissful emotional freedom. The support, guidance and empathy of a truly dedicated and compassionate counsellor guided me to heal into a new emotional blueprint for my life. My genuine hope is for people in our world to live lives free from anxiety, and to help light the path with hope, empathy, love and peace for your emotional freedom from anxiety. This is my sincere wish for you all.

May peace and love fill your world!

<u>*Peace*</u>

It does not mean to be in a place where there is no noise, trouble or hard work.

It means to be in the midst of those things and still be calm in your heart ("Peace it does not mean", (n.d.).

Table of Contents

Anxiety
–THE TORMENT

ANXIETY OVERRIDES ME, MY soul, my body, my very being!

The fear of this nervousness, placing me back to that place I hate again. Dread and despair take me over. Overwhelmed and panicked, desperately my body and mind remind me this is anxiety.

The aloneness, it engulfs me, fills me with fear and grips me with panic; I'm beside myself, like an out-of-body experience. The pounding of my racing heart is so fast I wish I could stop it. Please, somebody, anybody, help me!

My thoughts of giving up. Right here, right now, my pain would finally be over! This cruel fight for my survival in life, my hope fading, a cry from deep within my soul: please God, help me!

My Life with anxiety was an overwhelmingly crippling emotional state, which I so desperately tried to cope, function and exist in. The daily impact on our mental and physical wellbeing is somewhat unbearable at times. Feelings of hopelessness may start to consume our thoughts. Please hold on, have hope; there is a life free from anxiety, I promise you.

Counselling
-THE GOAT TRACK

THE DARKNESS CAME, ENGULFING me, surrounding me like the depths of the ocean on a dark and stormy day. Stuck in the middle of the abyss, I struggled for my life. Anxiety took hold of me, my conscious, my body and my very breath. No longer in control, the onset of this shock to my body filled me with fear. The panic set in; I was helpless again. Anxiety overtook me.

This part of my journey through counselling was very difficult to call a journey at the time. I would say to my counsellor, "I cannot call this a journey yet." A journey is meant to be a happy experience in your life, but dealing with your emotional trauma is not; it's confronting, exhausting and at times ruthlessly cruel. I understood why so many people stop and pull out altogether from counselling. To continue being challenged and confronted by the unknown, of what we'll find under each stone of our trauma, takes courage and vulnerability. I understand that the easier path to take in our life is to continue living with anxiety. To be free from anxiety takes courage, strength and determination—the absolute want to be free from it. To continue on the path of the unknown takes bravery. Sadly, this is why so many people stay living with anxiety. If I could allow you to feel life without anxiety and the freedom it brings, I can honestly say that you would not wait nor hesitate to unturn each stone of trauma in your life.

This journey through counselling, confronting our trauma in order to release our anxiety, can be incredibly challenging at times. Please be reassured it won't last forever. If I can conquer anxiety, anyone can. Just know there will also be times of joy and happiness along the way as well, I promise.

Most importantly, be realistic in understanding that working through our emotional states isn't always easy; it takes commitment, courage and time. Unfortunately, there is no magic wand to make this less painful or to make it go by faster. Be patient with counselling and with yourself, be kind to yourself, and remember anxiety isn't your fault. There are many strategies you can use to help yourself along the way. Choose whatever works and feels best for you. Please, grip onto your hope. As hard and lonely as this road may be, remind yourself there is freedom from anxiety.

Hope
–THE LIGHT!

THE LIGHT AT THE end of this tunnel is bright! So very bright you can hardly believe that some people have always lived in this way. How amazingly blessed they have been, and what we take for granted in our own lives at times is immeasurable to some of us. I feel so very blessed to have had such a beautifully authentic human being and counsellor walk by my side to the very end. Their support and guidance helped me enter into that light of freedom, transforming me in mind, body and spirit, helping me to find my truth, embrace it and become the person and woman I should have always been in life. The strength, hope and courage that bonded our relationship together through the mine fields of counselling encouraged and enabled me to continue on to the very end. I could not have survived this intense roller coaster ride of my life without you. My love, blessings and gratitude always.

Your hope will be your guiding light, pulling you along this path, on your way to emotional freedom. This hope transcends through the support and guidance of an authentically transparent counsellor. Trust and be guided by your own good judgment when finding a counsellor, someone who fits you. Your compatibility, level of comfort and honesty are paramount to the success of the journey through counselling. It's a commitment. Finding the right counsellor may take time; you may meet a few different counsellors before meeting the right one. Remember it has to be a workable relationship with your counsellor, enabling you to work through your trauma and anxiety. Go with your gut instinct on this; trust yourself to choose a counsellor who is right for you.

Happiness
-FREEDOM

THE TRAUMA IN MY life was a mountain to climb, the highest mountain I could imagine at times. The challenges I endured living with anxiety were many and painful. A pain and suffering I see today in so many people of this world. I realised through this life-changing journey that out of our trauma and suffering comes something so truly beautiful: a hope and a healing.

What waits for us through this healing is real happiness. A happiness that enables us to find our truth and purpose in life.

My strength, courage and determination to unturn every stone of trauma came from so desperately wanting to be free from my anxiety. The journey helped me to acknowledge, appreciate and understand what a real journey represents in our life. My beautiful sister-in-law once said, "a journey is to be always moving forward in our life," and she was right. It's a continuous emotional, healing, growing and moving forward process in life. It enables us to work through our pain and sadness as we journey through it. The journey may not always be easy, happy or fair, but in the end, if we learn to work through our trauma and pain, it will help us find our truths. To live life through our authentic true selves. I believe this is God's real purpose and plan for us in life. My journey helped me realise that all of us—every single one of us—has the ability to be free from anxiety, to live a happy and purposeful life. It's a choice of which path you take: the path of anxiety or the path to emotional freedom. The choice is yours.

We may reach a crossroads in our lives where we're not fully ready or committed to taking the path and journey into counselling. Working through our traumas and anxiety is confronting, challenging and sometimes incredibly lonely. I believe we all reach a point of desperation in our lives, of wanting to be free from the struggle and pain of anxiety. Be brave, have hope and commit yourself to the journey of being free from anxiety.

Blessings

Goodbye Anxiety – THE TOP OF THE MOUNTAIN

SO THIS IS EUPHORIA! I have reached the top of my mountain. This mountain of trauma, it's over! The climb was high—so very high at times—like walking on a cliff's edge, the rocks crumbling under my feet, falling to the unknown below, with God holding my hand. This is the only way I can describe my journey through counselling, the journey that released me from anxiety. The trauma from within me during this time was challenging, so challenging at times I felt I was hanging onto my life by a thread. What awaited me at the top of that mountain was a stillness so pure, an enlightenment, a freedom and real happiness. A lightness from within me that was so very free in spirit, it's nearly impossible to imagine. A forgiveness of my mind and body. A euphoric emotional release that brought peace to my soul.

Reaching this place of euphoria, to have finally worked through the trauma and anxiety, is not only liberating; it's a freeness, a completeness of our mind and body. A union and a balance, a calmness within us. An intertwining, a place I wish for us all to reach and embrace. *Amen*

Grief
– THE LETTING GO

 letting go that you'll feel once you've worked through your anxiety.

It's a sense of loss, a grief that you experience for a short time. Situations where you would normally feel anxious you won't, but you will feel other emotions, just on their own, not a mixed-up bundle of anxiety anymore. It's a genuine feeling of frustration, waiting to feel that anxiety again. Remember, it's a very real adjustment for your mind and body to be without the anxiety.

What I realised is that anxiety is a combination of emotions. Once your anxiety is worked through, it untangles and separates these emotions in order for you to function normally again. Hopefully having an awareness of this will help to elevate and support you through the adjustment of living without anxiety. The time frame for how long this adjustment takes will vary from person to person. For myself, who had a mountain of trauma over a prolonged period, I only experienced it a few times before it was completely gone.

My beautiful daughter once put it perfectly: I miss the feeling of anxiety; it's weird and frustrating not to feel it anymore! It sounds bizarre I know, just please remember to be patient with yourself. Understand that it takes time to completely adjust and heal from anxiety.

Love Yourself

LOVE YOURSELF AND HOLD onto hope. Know that you are not alone in your fight for survival and personal struggle with anxiety. A beautiful friend once said to me, "it's nice to know I'm not alone anymore; you feel so completely alone with anxiety." It's true there's an emptiness inside of you, a loneliness that no one and nothing can fill. You could literally be surrounded be people who love you, but nothing can take away the loneliness you feel with anxiety, nothing!

You may get to a point at different times in life where you have had enough of the struggle, you feel you want to give up and even maybe on life itself. Please don't. Have hope; you have a choice! Reaching this crossroad in your life gives you that choice. You can take life by the handle of hope and be finally free from anxiety, or you can take the handle of fear and continue on with the struggle.

Always remember, hope is knowing there's a light at the end of this tunnel with real freedom. Our fear may try to take over; we may start to lose hope; our light may start to fade, overridden by anxiety. Don't allow the anxiety to rule you or your life anymore. Remember it is just an emotional state attached to a trauma, which, with the right support, can be worked through and completely overcome.

You are strong! Having lived this long with anxiety, you're a survivor! Keep surviving and take the first step onto the path of freedom and into the light of hope. Our first step to change is to acknowledge the want to be free from the anxiety. You already have the courage, strength and determination to be free from it. You've had it all along to survive this struggle for as long as you have. If I could walk your path for you, believe me I would. Having experienced the reality of being free from anxiety, I know it's real. My wish for everyone living with anxiety is that you experience the weightlessness and freedom of being totally free from anxiety, to find your true self, your truth, and purpose in life.

LIFE'S PURPOSE

I BELIEVE WE ALL have our own purpose in life, a purpose that was made for each and every one of us. For me, surviving my mountain of trauma and overcoming anxiety happened for this very purpose: to write this book, to give back hope and healing, to help people become emotionally free from anxiety and to find truth and purpose in life.

Be open to what your purpose is once you are free from your anxiety. It's a calling in our lives, like a thread that pulls at you. Be open to this; listen and pay attention. Opportunities that come our way happen and are presented to us in life for a reason: to put us on the right path in life and to help us find our purpose.

Most importantly, love yourself! I believe this is a gift from God. Externally our love helps us love others; internally our love helps us love ourselves. Love helps us open up the door to our true selves, the way we are meant to live our lives, with love!

Loving one another brings us together; love unites us as humans, as friends, as family, as communities, as nations and as a *world*. Unity brings peace, and with peace comes healing. Please help bring peace and healing into our world by sharing this book with someone you love.

Hope, healing and peace. Namaste

Florence Nightingale

MY LIFE... SHOWED HOW a woman of very ordinary ability has been led by God in strange an unaccustomed paths to do in his service what he has done in her. And if I could tell you all, you would see how God has done all, and I nothing. I have worked hard, very hard, that is all; and I have never refused God anything. (Sala, 2008, pp.61).

Through understanding, creates knowledge,
Unfolding wisdom and transforming
oneself in truth.

Blessings

Reference List

"Peace". (n.d.). Retrieved from https://www.passiton.com/inspirational-quotes/7228-peace-it-does-not-mean-to-be-in-a-place-where

Sala, D. (2008). *You are Blessed: Inspiration to Recharge your soul.* Barbour Publishing.

Credit: kaewta Sirimongkolwattana
Hand drawn Angel playing guitar
Coloured by: Ellie Simpson